A Weekly
Scotsman

David Daiches' other books include:

Robert Burns

Two Worlds (*autobiography*)

A Critical History of English Literature

The Paradox of Scottish Culture

God and the Poets

For B.
Who encouraged me
To write poetry again

COIA
22ⁿᵈ Feb
1994

A Weekly Scotsman

And Other Poems

David Daiches

With an autobiographical introduction
A foreword by George Bruce
And a frontispiece portrait of the author
By Emilio Coia

BLACK ACE BOOKS

First published in 1994 by
Black Ace Books
Duns, TD11 3SG, Scotland

© David Daiches 1994
Foreword © George Bruce 1994
Typography © Black Ace Editorial 1994

Typeset in Scotland by Black Ace Editorial

Printed in Great Britain by
Martins the Printers Ltd, Seaview Works
Spittal, Berwick upon Tweed, TD15 1RS

A CIP catalogue record for this book
is available from the British Library

ISBN (hardback) 1–872988–06–7
ISBN (paperback) 1–872988–11–3

The publishers gratefully acknowledge
subsidy from the Scottish Arts Council
towards the publication of this volume

Acknowledgements

Most of the 'Early Poems' were first published
either in *Poetry* (USA) or *The New Yorker*.

Poems in the later sections have appeared in
The Scotsman, *Aberdeen University Review*,
Chapman, and *Stand*.

I should like to thank my good friend
Emilio Coia for offering to do the drawing
of me for this book.

CONTENTS

Foreword

Surprised, we have every right to be, but now that we have this book it might be said of David Daiches, as poet, we might have predicted much that is here – the skill with words, the good-humoured urbanity, the alertness to nuances of meaning, the poetic response to speech rhythms which will give pleasure to every reader with an ear, and also a fluency of the imagination which takes us from cabbages to kings at a single breathing. Surprised we may be at his poetic self-denying ordinance in view of this production, but such qualities were implied in the generosity of his literary appreciations and reflections over the years, though his humour could not shine as it does here:

> Wishing I had a new line in wit

How unnecessary! He has it in abundance even as the poem, entitled 'Lines', ends:

> I write these few lines
> About lines.

And to arrive at these pay-off lines he has explored references of the word from 'Lines of communication, like railways, telephone wires', to 'the bottom line where everything stops like / the buck at the White House'.

Word curiosity is an interest, but there is a persistent deeper concern for truth to place and fact and experience, which yield is first encountered in 'Pathetic Fallacy', which begins with a delicate evocation of the scene:

> Mist on the Downs. The garden end obscured.
> The trees stand faintly out against the white.
> A muted scene, at rest, complete, assured,
> Matter of lines, relationships and light.

The last line hints that the impact on the nervous system is under inspection. The line that follows makes the position clear:

> There is no meaning in the stance of trees.

The scruple of imposing meaning on nature does not preclude the idea of meaning in life. The poem ends:

> Our one imperative: as we slowly fall
> Down to the final dissolution, know
> We touch the earth with meaning as we go.

Now David Daiches absorbs into his verse the condition that gave his lectures and writings their generosity; as expressed in 'Seasons':

> Look back, look forward,
> All that mixed texture of the searching mind
> That keeps us human.

It is, perhaps, the unexpected in poetry that matters most. We find it especially near the end of the book – as when in 'Flowers and Grocers', David, then young, takes a friend of ninety-two years 'a drive in the car', who was 'Touched by the ordinariness'. The poem ends:

> Now myself well past the Psalmist's span
> Of seventy years I often think of this
> And feel, surprisingly, a surge of love
> For flowers and grocers everywhere.

The extra-ordinariness is not only in the 'surge of love' but in the giving of a ranging context to the experience, even in the reference to 'Psalmist'. This ranging allows for running from the comical to the serious and to the reverse. In 'Descent' we are simply, apparently, with children 'sledging into the dusk', but it is 'the Bruegel landscape' though they go 'down the slope that borders the Bow Butts', and while there is 'Light. Fall. Darkness.' . . .

> Far off in the Gulf they are preparing for war,
> Tanks rehearse in the desert, in sand, not snow,
> But here in this Scottish village the children
> Descend the snowy slopes with laughter into darkness.

Here is the dearest continuity. In Bruegel Icarus falls from the sky and the common business of ploughing and shepherding goes on as the true miracle. Here in David Daiches the 'surge of love' continues for the children, and for the strangeness of human life.

There must be more of this poetry to come. I am privileged to write some words about it.

George Bruce
February 1994

Introduction

I cannot remember a time when I was not interested in playing with rhymes and rhythms.

I was about nine years old when I decided that I was going to become a great poet. Soon after the establishment of a Children's Hour in the old British Broadcasting Company's Edinburgh station 2EH I sent one of my poems to 'Auntie Molly' of that programme and she read it out on the air. My father noted my interest in writing verse and one day sat down beside me at the dining-room table – again, when I was nine years old – and explained the nature of metrical feet, with their names, scanning various examples of verse and marking the stressed and unstressed syllables.

I was eleven when the school magazine *The Watsonian* published a poem of mine, an exercise in trochaic metre, entitled 'To a Fountain in Moonlight' (a sight I had never seen) in alternately rhyming lines beginning:

> Gleaming showers, gently spraying
> Up into the air.

That is all I can remember, and the copy of the magazine that printed it has long since disappeared.

At the age of fourteen I founded, edited and produced by hand (two copies of each issue, one with carbon paper) a magazine called *The Family Entertainer*, of which I wrote the entire contents. There were about a dozen numbers. The early issues contained comic poems and parodies, together with stories and allegedly funny articles. I had been reading the poetry of Edward Lear and Lewis Carroll, and enjoyed writing what I called 'nonsense verse'. One such poem, 'The Pollywagoo', began as follows:

Where palm trees are waving
And madmen are raving
And Dutch Bands of Hope souls of Dutchmen are saving,
Where the moon's ever blue
And the Pole Star is too
That's the place where you'll find the great Pollywagoo.

O he isn't a bird and he isn't a beast
And he isn't an insect or fish in the least:
He lives not in water, he lives not in air,
And his cave's in a country called Goodness Knows Where;
But if you ever see
One of these up a tree
Let me tell you that he has no right to be there.

There were four more verses.

I also wrote parodies of the poems we studied in our English class at school, the most notable being 'The Rime of the Ancient Scavenger', which told the sad tale of a former hotel chef whose disaster with a cake led to his losing his job and taking to a life of scavenging. It opened:

It was an ancient scavenger
Who walked along the road,
His beard was long, his nose was red,
He wore a dustbin on his head
In which his hair was stowed.

And, as he came along the street,
He paused and heaved a sigh,
And round about the neighb'ring pubs
He cast his glittering eye.
And as he saw a man come out
He raised his voice and gave a shout,
A very weird cry . . .

But I also took myself seriously as a poet. In my middle teens I wrote a series of long melancholy poems in Spenserian stanzas collectively entitled *Tristia*. I wrote dozens of sonnets, both of the Italian and English variety, and experimented with rime-royal and terza-rima. Then, when we read *The Lady of the Lake* and *Marmion* at school, I developed a passion for narrative verse and wrote a long poem on the exploits of Judas Maccabeus modelled on *Marmion* in style and metre, even to the extent of including reflective personal passages between each canto and inserting incidental lyrics. Most of these works I destroyed at the end of my first year at university, after reading Hopkins, Eliot and the early Auden, in the belief that all I had hitherto written was old-fashioned romantic trash. I am sorry now, for some of it was (I flatter myself) technically accomplished.

I never gave up light verse, however. At the age of sixteen I rendered the first book of the *Odyssey* into limerick verse, deliberately choosing the most non-epic metre for an epic story, to see what would happen. It began:

Tell me O Muse of the chap
Who wandered all over the map.
This remarkable boy
After bashing down Troy
Started off on a tour of mishap.

As a student I wrote both serious and comic poems for *The Student*, then an ambitious fortnightly magazine. I remember a 'Study in Triple Rhyme', which began:

Listen all while I narrate how once in far Nairobi a
Black man was bitten by a dog and died of hydrophobia . . .

And I translated into English verse some of the poems in John Purves' anthology of Italian poetry that we studied in the Italian class, winning the class prize for Italian verse translation. In

1933 I edited for the University English Literature Society a collection of student poems in which Robert Garioch (then R.G. Sutherland) and Sorley (then Sammy) Maclean first appeared. My own contributions included two Edinburgh poems, one of which was simply four lines:

> As I came down through Potterrow
> The sun rose red above the roofs.
> 'How strange,' I thought, 'I didn't know
> The sun could rise in Potterrow.'

(This was an early-morning winter scene in the old Potterrow, before they pulled it down.)

In my student days I continued to believe that my destiny was to be a poet, but somehow I got drawn more and more into writing *about* literature – I was doing 'honours English' at the University – and after winning the Vans Dunlop scholarship which enabled me to go on to Oxford, to become the first Bradley Fellow of Balliol, I found myself in an academic career without having planned or even wished for it.

When I was teaching at the University of Chicago – the circumstances that took me there are explained in my autobiographical books *Two Worlds* and *A Third World* – I still wrote poetry and contributed regularly to the Chicago periodical *Poetry*. After the war, when I spent five years as professor at Cornell University, I contributed both poetry and stories to the *New Yorker* and continued doing so sporadically in my subsequent years teaching at Cambridge.

My books, however, were critical and historical. I was drawn more and more into that kind of writing and gradually I realised that I was not a 'poet' – in the sense of being committed primarily, passionately and continuously to writing poetry – but a literary critic and historian who wrote occasional verse. At the same time I regarded much of the verse published in little magazines as sloppy meanderings with no real craftsmansip or artistic form and I was dismayed at the way in which this kind of undisciplined self-indulgence so often passed for poetry, as it still does. I sent to a New York poetry magazine a bit of meaningless verbal doodling, composed in a matter of seconds, and they printed it, thanking me for my 'distinguished contribution'.

Not that I objected to the modern movement in poetry. One of my earliest essays, which appeared in a collection of essays entitled *New Literary Values* I published when I was twenty-three, was entitled 'Gerard Manley Hopkins and the Modern Poets'. In America I conducted seminars on Yeats and Eliot and lectured on Auden and his contemporaries. My great passion was Joyce, on whose work I conducted a graduate seminar at Chicago, and I came to know *Ulysses* almost by heart. I recognized in Joyce a fascination with language that had haunted me since childhood and is reflected in my book *Was*. For me, however, all art was order, form, pattern, and aimless 'splairging' was the antithesis of art. For whatever reason, I wrote less and less verse and emerged, to my surprise, as a scholar and critic. This is not what I intended for myself as a youngster.

My poetic career was thus in four phases: my childhood imitations, experiments and parodies; my adolescent mood pieces; my more sophisticated efforts (influenced at first by the later Yeats) when I was teaching at American universities; and finally, in my retirement, a new surge of verse-writing in a variety of moods and forms. This book presents a selection from the two latter of these phases. It is very far from fulfilling my childhood ambitions, which envisaged a shelf-full of 'poetical works', but I hope it will afford some pleasure.

David Daiches
February 1994

Early Poems

To Kate, Skating Better
Than Her Date

Wait, Kate! You skate at such a rate
You leave behind your skating mate.
Your splendid speed won't you abate?
He's lagging far behind you, Kate.
He brought you on this skating date
His shy affection thus to state,
But you on skating concentrate
And leave him with a woeful weight
Pressed on his heart. Oh what a state
A man gets into, how irate
He's bound to be with life and fate
If, when he tries to promulgate
His love, the loved one turns to skate
Far, far ahead to demonstrate
Superior speed and skill. Oh hate
Is sure to come of love, dear Kate,
If you so treat your skating mate.
Turn again, Kate, or simply wait
Until he comes, then him berate
(Coyly) for catching up so late
For Kate, he *knows* your skating's great,
He's *seen* your splendid figure eight,
He is not in here to contemplate
Your supersonic skating rate –
That is not why he made the date.
He's anxious to expatiate
Oh how he wants you for his mate.
And don't you want to hear him, Kate?

From 'Six War Poems' (1942)

Fall from the slow-drawn days like melting wax,
Uncomfortable fear. Drip softly from
The hanging boughs of eyeless trees, insist
On entry through defying stable doors,
Oozing through straw, leering from dusty roofs.
Advance to music, fouling thoroughfares,
Corrupting homesteads, while the fungoid breath
Of a diseased fate warms the chill-faced world.
These are mushrooms where snowdrops grew.
The sky which once showed stars is now obscene
With buttons. O descend, festering fear,
Speak your appointed lines, play out your part,
That the kind curtain may at last appear,
Reminding us the story was not true.
Leaving the theatre, let us then demand
The northern blast, lift up the eyes and hail
The distant gelid isles where the aloof polar bear
Pushes his whiskered nose into the frozen world
To see the sun glinting on ice, the blanched earth aseptic,
And, far below, the icicled grottos blue and silent
Leading down, down into the dark where strange beasts dwell
And the shivering wind creeps through cracks invisible;
Where the quick blizzard falls, shutting out sight,
Hurriedly covering the bones of lost heroes,
Soundless patter of myriad feet descending,
Tap-dancing lightly on the graves they filled;
Where the solemn penguin bows to the midnight sun
And sometimes the gleam and crackle of northern lights
Makes pageant for a public that never comes,
Fireworks for small boys who are not there to see,
Scoop for staff-photographer who has not been informed;

Where six-months night hangs chill over the slush-gray desert
Bringing the fearless winds to cry through the dark,
Clutching the hypnotized earth with cold, skinny fingers,
Hollow-faced ice witch mastering the land.

On with the play, hot fear,
That we may soon
Turn backs upon the velvet stage and go
Alive into the tonic night.

Back in Time to Make Lunch

Oft he to her his charge of quick return
Repeated, shee to him as oft engag'd
To be return'd by Noon amid the Bow'r
And all things in best order to invite
Noontide repast. – Paradise Lost, *Book IX.*

We know what happened. That lunch was never made,
And Adam watched in vain for Eve's return.
Somebody came – we know her – Helen, perhaps,
Ophelia, Cleopatra, Guinevere,
All that sad rout of tainted heroines
Thinking by lovely gestures to conceal
That loss, that long-lost lunch;
Covering by love or lust or sacrifice
That long-lamented loss,
By love or lust or burning topmost towers
To hide that lost lunch and those faded flowers
That slipped from Adam's hand.
Hark to the mockingbird, the cheers, the band.

The tinkle of that distant dinner-bell
Echoes in mortal ears, and frozen peas
Still fail to interpose a little ease
Or silence murmurs from that earlier war –
Ancestral voices prophesying more.

What cunning Paradises have we here?
Where flew the primal birds, the engines fly;
Where grew the lush grass, now the cactus burns.
This is no sea to scan with shaded eye
For the returning sailor; he returns
No sailor but a leering buccaneer.
Home at last is the hunter, home from the hill;
He went out Jacob, comes back Esau still.

All were successful; all left large bequests
To feather scores of post-lapsarian nests
And pay philosophers to count the cost –
That lunch unmade, that bliss undone, that garden lost.

Pathetic Fallacy

Mist on the Downs. The garden end obscured.
The trees stand faintly out against the white.
A muted scene, at rest, complete, assured,
Matter of lines, relationships and light.

There is no meaning in the stance of trees.
Here is a truth we must undo: we must
Implicate nature in our reveries;
We need a neutral world to bear our trust;
We press our burdens on indifferent things.
Take that, and that! How unsolicited
Our gifts, what help the giving brings
To giver: out of need is fancy bred,
Till even the wind acquires a human call.

Our one imperative: as we slowly fall
Down to the final dissolution, know
We touch the earth with meaning as we go.

Thoughts on a Thaw

This is the third day since Thursday that
    the thermometer has stood
Steady at thirty. Soft snow thrust through sad skies,
Sending its thousand snowflakes thronging on thatch
    and sidewalk,
Supernal throwaway sifting over thresholds. See it
    spread on thicket,
Shining on thorn and shrub, sequestering thorp and suburb.
Though I thought the snow, so thick it stood,
    would stay through a set season,
Three short, if thriving, sessions seemed sufficient,
    for someone, I think, has sensed a thaw.
Some subtle thaumaturgy has sent a thousand signs
Signalling shift from spreading thaw, therapeutic
    of soil and smirch,
Thesaurus of softness, to thrumming water splash,
    threat of soaking.
I think this shift is strange, seeing no theory to solve
These seasonal subtleties, sudden thermal shifts.
Some seem thankful for this thaw. The more thoughtful,
Thinking of slush, see no thrill but suffer throes of sadness,
Sad threnody of thwarted skiers sounds, thrasonic
    skaters sigh –
No splendid showing off for them in thaw.

Myself, I suffer snow with sullen thought,
And sing this song for thaw.

1947

Weighing the ages makes a social game:
Simple to blame and praise resistless dead,
'Choose it,' he said, 'leaf back time's dirty pages,
Choose your pet days and seriously name
The time you'd best have lived. Pick one,' he said.

The trim past beckons: we select a sire,
Spenser's brave courtier, eighteenth–century squire,
Victorian rebel, early Christian or
Rupert Brooke before the First World War.

Live without sulfa drugs? No anaesthesia?
When sweethearts died for lack of penicillin?
When surgeons' tools were full of germs and dirt?
When sex was warped and even dentists hurt?

All pyramids rest on inarticulate sorrows
But still it can be cosy at the top
Where sit the wise and kindly gentlemen
Free to be good, privileged to inquire,
Released to search for truth. Nice to be there.
Plato had slaves, and may I even doubt
If Christ did his own laundry?

Queen Anne wits lauded Homer, but they knew
The world had blossomed for their happy few.
Serene by candlelight the sceptic Hume
Sipped claret in his well-appointed room.
Macaulay welcomed progress. Robert Browning
Managed to keep his faith alive by clowning.
Adam took comfort: and from Egypt land
Purposeful Moses led his interested band.

And here we are, full of potential bliss,
Crying in chorus: 'Anything but this!'

Winter Song

When I walk home through snow or slush
Under a dismal sky,
I do not seek to question much
The what and/or the why.
I am contented to observe
A wintry world. I keep my nerve.

I steer my course mid frozen rocks,
I forbear to shiver;
Ice cubes as big as city blocks
Beckon me from the river.
I answer them as they deserve,
Displaying how I keep my nerve.

I tell the truth – I am no fibber –
And loudly cry to all
That though the ghouls of winter gibber
And mock the buried Fall,
From mental calm I do not swerve –
I swallow hard, but keep my nerve.

Why do they look at me askance
As though my nerve had failed?
I do not live in gloomy trance,
My cheek has never paled.
I shout to all, without reserve,
'*I keep my nerve, I keep my nerve.*'

Historical Footnote

The Hussite schism by the time of Zizka's death was, as with our knowledge of what has happened since then we can see, inexpugnable, whether by Sigismund, Cardinal Beaufort or Cardinal Cesarini, by the wiles of the Council of Basle, by the assault of Pius II and Matthias Corvinus, or the craft of Ferdinand I. – From a review of John Zizka and the Hussite Revolution *in the* Times Literary Supplement *(1956).*

I see refracted through a prism
The truth about the Hussite schism,
And so I think that I can risk a
Note on conditions after Zizka.
(The Pope thought him a thug; a bull
Left his views inexpugnable.)
Sigismund raved, with naught to show for't,
And vainly thundered Cardinal Beaufort;
Nor was the smallest, teeny-weeny
Effect achieved by Cesarini;
Nor could a deft Conciliar snarl
Aimed at the Hussite schism from Basle
Destroy it. Further, those who reckoned
That the assault of Pius Second
Would wreck it – why, they just rehearsed
The failure of Ferdinand the First.
Pius in fact proved just as minus
A quantity as did Corvinus.

Well, well, this is a frightful fuss
To make about the views of Huss.

Sing a Song of Symmetry

If the Sea had been drawn round the Earth in regular figures and borders, it might have been a great Beauty to our Globe, and we should have reasonably concluded it a work of the first Creation, or of Nature's first production; but finding on the contrary all the marks of disorder and disproportion in it, we may as reasonably conclude, that it did not belong to the first order of things, but was something succedaneous, when the degeneracy of mankind, and the judgments of God had destroy'd the first World, and subjected the Creation to some kind of Vanity. – The Sacred Theory of the Earth, *by Thomas Burnet (edition of 1684).*

Burnet! You wring my heart full sore.
I had not realised before
How crooked, twisted, bent and curled
Is this our poor, distorted world.
I look below and at my feet
I see misshapen grasses meet.
Above me, in the endless sky,
The malformed clouds float sadly by.
I eye my limbs. What grim surprises!
Fingers and toes of different sizes!
I don't like this at all; it rankles.
My calves are thicker than my ankles.
How can such disproportion please?
And what is one to make of knees?
No comfort, none. I must confess
The human form is just a mess;
And animals – let me be terse –
Are, on reflection, even worse,
While sky and meadow, field and tree
Are just as ugly as can be.
Enough! I shut my burdened eyes
And do my best to visualise

A world where all is neatly framed
And Burnet need not be ashamed.
Ah, in this ideal world I see
Nothing so monstrous as a tree.
But o'er her surface Nature drapes
Some pleasing vegetable shapes;
No rudely disproportioned storms
Distort their geometric forms;
If any breeze their limbs inclines,
They keep to parallel straight lines.
The world of living creatures shares
This zeal for perfect rounds and squares.
The worm that wriggles in the soil
Moves neatly in a single coil.
Well-patterned dogs with cube-shaped muzzles,
Checked with squares like crossword puzzles,
Symmetric pigs whose shapely hams
Form perfect parallelograms –
Such ordered creatures play their part
In boosting their Creator's art.
How trim the patterned ocean strand
In perfect squares of yellow sand!
I note the rocks that bound the seas –
Triangular (isosceles).
Neat fishes as they swim adduce
The square of the hypotenuse,
And I observe the shapes of clams
Like Euclid's finest diagrams.

A nymph approaches – creature fair!
How straight and even is her hair!
Her eyes two perfect circles are;
Her bosom is rectangular.
Am I delighted? I am not!
– Burnet, you talk the damnedest rot.

Final Thoughts on the Weather
in England in 1953

The bright earth moves in destined grooves:
The speed of light remains the same,
The full moon's rise is no surprise –
All is predictable and tame.
When Isaac Newt was bumped by fruit
The speed at which his apple sped
Was neither less nor more, I guess,
Than that which bumps a modern head.
No physicist has ever missed
The permanence of nature's laws;
Astronomers will all aver
That wandering planets never pause;
The doctors know – they'll tell you so –
That measles always has a rash,
That if you fall from something tall
There's bound to be a nasty smash.
It takes no skill to know that ill
Will come from drinking gin in quarts
Or if you take ground glass in cake
You'll soon be feeling out of sorts.
There is no flaw in Mendel's law,
And Euclid's propositions yet
Refer to truths that modern youths
Are not permitted to forget.

Wise men and fools are bound by rules;
The universe is standardized;
The universe's primal curse
Is that it cannot be surprised.
Its laws are strict, we can predict
What x will do when faced by y;
It's got a norm, it's uniform,
It doesn't change and doesn't try.
There's only one way it can act –
And that's a sci-en-ti-fic fact!

Yet here in England, months together,
Nobody can predict the weather.

The Laloc Trees

Well into the nineteenth century many pronunciations survived that people would now think laughable. Lord Ernest Hamilton tells us, in Forty Years On, *that in the sixties: 'Septuagenarians might still be heard describing how "The dear dook was obleeged by the heat to set in a gyarden cheer, under the laloc trees, drinking tay out of yellow chaney coops, while his leddy on the balcóny ate cowcumbers and reddishes off goold plates brought to Oxfordsheer from Roome."'* – The English Language, *by Ernest Weekley.*

Still standing are the laloc trees;
The spacious lawn is trim and neat,
No longer trod by dookal feet
But kept by Whitehall employees.

The cheer on which His Grace would doze
Lies mouldering in the gyarden shed,
And all the gyardeners are dead
Who bred the special dookal rose.

Obleeged by stiffening tax demands
And sadly short of needed goold,
The heir's ancestral feeling cooled;
He placed the house in other hands.

The nation owns the stately hall
Where once a duchess sipped her tay;
Where once a coronet held sway
A civil servant governs all.

From the balcóny you may see
A view of all of Oxfordsheer;
The visitors will stand and peer
And scan the prospect (for a fee).

Where cowcumbers once grew in frames
You now will see a painted sign:
'Tea served in garden, two-and-nine'.
Democracy asserts its claims.

The dook lies silent in the tomb,
And eager tourists come in troops
To view his yallow chaney coops
And goolden plates that came from Roome.

Observation Car

I know a man who rubbernecks the past.
Tourist with guide, he notes each signal sight –
It's there, it's happened, anyone can cast
His eye on it, where all is *was*, not *might*.
Observe him seated by his labelled files,
Facing with firmness the recorded years,
Brave connoisseur of the receding miles,
The tracks of other people's hopes and fears.
Ah, retrograde's the way. Look back, look back,
The past lies all before us, plain to see,
And all our yesterdays create the track
Which measures miles where people used to be.
Today is what tomorrow will have shown:
Ride backward towards the will-have-been unknown!

Paradise Mislaid

It happened all the time when I was young.
There was a bay beyond the Point, and there,
I knew, were sands true gold and rocks
Shining in sunlight, fish sporting in pools,
And the air brighter, brighter. When I turned
The corner of the cliff to face it, it was gone:
A low, flat stretch of sea-weed took its place.
I was used to such magic. So gardens moved
And the gate opened on dull, plain yards;
So, behind fences, shining rivers turned
To slag heaps, and great gleaming railways, high
With promise of adventure, turned as I came
To mean streets with the children kicking cans
And the dustbins rampant. If I had not known
That this was trickery, not truth; cheap joke
By pranking angel who enjoyed his game
Of dropping curtains over beaches, gardens,
Railways I was after; teasing us with hide-and-seek;
I might have thought at last that Paradise
Was a device to keep us from despair,
And then despaired to recognise it so.
But I could tell a joke – even a sour one –
From a disaster: all the while I knew
Mislaid is not lost, to tease is not to damn.
But is it, is it? The jest keeps up so long.
Should I report the prankster as delinquent?
If so, to whom? And then perhaps (but I
Must not believe it) I got it wrong, all wrong,
And nobody was teasing after all.

A Weekly Scotsman

Monday

Monday, Mournday, bears the sorrows of the world,
It marches on relentless, moving in a murky motion.
'Dull today,' the countryman said, passing me on the road,
Bearing his portion of the dull day with mindless dignity.
Maybe meaningful Monday markets make money
For many merchants. Not mine
This cash consolation. But mine this world, alas,
This Monday world that shows the sorry smear
Of labour, loss and endless lack of love:
Come to terms with Monday and you know
The grit and grime of all those other lives.
It is the test. Connect
With Monday's message
And share in all those other sadnesses.

Tuesday

More fluent, perhaps, a Tuesday poem
    than a Monday,
Softly falling across the inclined ear.
Monday's words were sad and separate,
Dull-coloured too, as befits the start of a workaday
    world,
But Tuesday – linger over the first syllable,
    draw it out
Tyoos-day, Tyoooosday, limpid and flowing
Promises a new kind of life.
What?
Not 'what', that flat explosion, but 'how',
    long-drawn, musical.
How shall we draw out Tuesday? Choose it in summer,
Salmon and white wine and strawberries in the garden.
O Tuesday, be yourself, fulfil your promise.
Your colour is sky-blue, your music the violin,
    your pace a gliding motion.
Elsewhere the Mondays gather, sullen and grey,
Reminding of famine and war and national disasters.
The world is crowded with Mondays making their
    moral demands.
Stay a while with Tuesday, indulgent.

Wednesday

What is the 'd' doing clogging up this day?
Wodan's day you clarify, but we say Wensday,
Avoiding the dull thud of 'd' and any sign of wedding day.
D-Day, but I pronounce you D-less, the great Wen.
Wensday athwart the middle of the week
Looks Janus-like, both backward and in front,
A hump-backed bridge, a middleman, a bindweed,
A day for compromise, probably brown in colour,
A necessary day, or weeks would fall apart.
O necessary Wednesday, hebdomadal lynch-pin,
All hail, all rain, all snow
That falls of Wednesday
Moistens the week and keeps it live.
There now good Wensday, take this comfort,
    talk to your friends
On either side. For you replenish them.

Thursday

Thursday is many-featured,
Holy on Maundy or the week-end's first whisper.
I sailed from Thurso on a Thursday once
To Orkney, the day fitting the town, I thought,
With Thursday weather, cloudy but clearing.
What promises there lay in Thursday then!
Good Thursday, speak again of better things,
Sound your promissory notes like Cuckoo's springtime noise
As you move on from dawn to thirsty noon
Leading to opening time.
Resourceful Thursday, open to suggestions,
Tolerant and changing Thursday, I pass on you
A suspended sentence, hanging in air
With chord of an unfinished symphony
Like – like – and then again unlike . . .
No coda here.

Friday

Friday is yellow like field of buttercups.
Don't ask me why: I know.
Streaming from school on Friday I felt its brightness,
And now with school long faded
I savour its freedom still.
Friday, my day, day of fried fish, fried day,
Let others think of crucifixion, eating fish
In sorrow. This was and is
The day of liberation.
Ah, freedom is a noble thing
This butter-coloured day.
Friday, enjoy your fish.

Saturday

Crown of the week, fair Saturday,
Queen of the days, not saturnine at all,
But dancing. Allegro ma non troppo,
Musical Saturday, O could we hear you
Da capo, but no:
Unless the rolling days moved on
You could not bear your bright and dancing role.
So roll on days, and every seventh
Bring back Queen Saturday, our dancing girl.

Sunday

Sunday demands more formal verse upon it,
And so I end this series with a sonnet.

Sunday in Scotland, sermon-long it was,
Indoors and closed: no sun on Sunday then,
No secular activities because
The day belonged to God and not to men.
(We talked of men in those benighted days
And thoughtlessly included women too:
The males devised the forms of prayer and praise,
Male world, male day, male order in the pew.)
And now the Sunday supermarket reigns,
And shirt-sleeved man with lazy-trousered wife
Trundles the trolley, counts domestic gains,
And all that fallen world has come to life.
Law and the Profits: scriptural re-grading:
In Parliament they call it Sunday trading.

Meals

Breakfast

*It is a sharp word, 'Breakfast', like 'break step' when
crossing a bridge. And break fast, no time to lose.*

A cold school morning, my mother ill,
My father in his dressing-gown
Bent over stove, stirring with spirtle the porridge.
Ah the great fight to rise from the warm sheets
And face a schoolday. The water was cold for washing,
The kitchen fire (which heated it) just lit.
Three of us round the battered kitchen table,
And porridge, cocoa, wedges of buttered bread.
(I thought of buttered toast as fanciful,
Toast was for tea-time, toasted at the fire
With long expanding fork.)
Sometimes I finished homework over breakfast,
Propping a book on milk-jug, reading about
French verbs or German rivers.
The adult joy of breakfast lingering
Not for the schoolboy. Not for him
Café complet or croissants. No succo d'arancia,
Coffee and rolls on warm Italian balconies.
A rigorous workaday meal, but at weekend slower
    though not lavish.
I have seen
Film-stars in elegant wraps on patios,
'More coffee darling?' That was at the pictures,
The U.S. rich dawdling in moneyed ease.
Coffee they drank. *We* moved from cocoa
To grown-up tea. Coffee for the Continent,
Its smell my earliest continental smell
    (with French tobacco).

Then, now fully adult, the English hotel breakfast,
Not the thin continental but the full English,
Compulsory eating since paid for anyway.
English? Ah, but the true Scottish breakfast,
Porridge of course, kippers or Arbroath smokies,
And Dundee marmalade. Oatcakes,
Kebbuck. Eggs of course unlimited.
(I'm thinking of a farm near Foggieloan.)
They used to eat their porridge standing up
Like Israelites awaiting exodus.
Prince Charlie breakfasted
On whisky and a piece of bread
Before Culloden.

Lunch

Lunch was a paper bag with two jeelie pieces
Eaten in the playground. A slight repast
Taken between two meal-times says the OED.
Fair enough, but swallowed with a cup of Miss Thyne's cocoa
From the school lunch-room and, greatly daring,
Two ha'penny doughnuts from the counter tin,
One could not call it slight. The seagulls
Who swooped down for the crumbs did not feel slighted.
Quantum mutatus ab illo, lunch with wine and napery
    as a guest at Lords,
Food and drink dominating the wicket.
Or consider the lunch-room in a small provincial hotel,
With steak-and-kidney pie and apple tart,
Or the ubiquitous bar lunch, revolution of our time,
Or haughty luncheons in marquees,
Or that strange lunch the wedding breakfast,
    digested with best man's jokes.
Lorry drivers in roadside cafés eating huge platefuls
Of bacon and eggs. No slight repast for these.
Lunch, I respect your versatility,
I hail you in my lunch-break,
Many-dimensioned lunch.
What is your symbol, your defining sign?
Perhaps
Suspended on the door an inky note
GONE TO LUNCH.

Tea

Bread-and-butter first, then cucumber sandwiches,
Only then a small cake followed by a chocolate biscuit.
A tea-party, ceremonial:
Delicate china, a cake-basket, genteel guests
   crooking their little
   fingers.
Then the more robust teas, with massive scones and jam
Or the high tea with finnan haddie and unlimited bread
   and baps and cream cookies.
A special treat: tea in P.T.'s, with the tea-room music
   playing, ladies with their stringed instruments,
Or tea at the zoo, after a ride on the young elephant.
And at the Banffshire local show
The proud official announcing:
'Will all members of the commytée,
That is, all commíttee members,
Who have not yet partaken of tea
Kindly report at the tea-tent
And oblige.'
Teasing memories indeed, mixed with Alice
   and the mad hatter and the doormouse.
In the cottage window a little placard: 'Teas'.

Dinner

Soup ladled from a tureen, one splash per plate,
Then slurped from a large soup-spoon, sideways.
Meat, potatoes, cauliflower, solid fare,
A pie to follow perhaps, or a steamy pudding.
Day's crowning stuffing for the middle class.
Workmen had midday dinner brought with them
   in bags and boxes,
Consumed on building sites or inside vans,
Huge sandwiches with gulped hot thermos drinks.
Dinner in Oxbridge colleges with black-suited servants
Attending. 'You are taking wine, Sir?'
Cunning competitive talk by Fellows, throw-away wit,
Residue of an indulged monastic life.
Afterwards the port, circling clockwise,
Candlelight on the red-filled glasses,
The cracking of nuts, of jokes, of reputations.
Guests assembled for dinner in country houses,
Pre-prandial sherry, arranged pairing of partners,
A Henry James world.
Or the humbler dinner party:
'Come to dinner on Thursday.' What shall we give them?
Something French perhaps? Try out that recipe.
An unpretentious
But worthy little wine: chap at the office recommended it.
   What do you think?
So we play social games, putting a little ceremony
Into our friendships. Eating together,
The primal social gesture.

Or the discreet dinner for two
In the alcove, eating and drinking for love,
Courting by feeding.
The railway dining-car,
Upper-class meals on wheels.
The scenery rolls by, the soup moves sideways
On the plate. The conjuring attendant
Balances deftly with prestidigious skill,
Then the man comes to write the bill, enormous.
A man is rich, said Dr. Johnson,
If he can see ahead to his next dinner.

Addendum

Fish suppers are a common thing,
Haddock or whiting, cod or ling.
Well chewed, well savoured, down it slips
Accompanied of course by chips.
Its presence you can always tell
In streets by the seductive smell.
I won't in any manner slight
A meal that gives so much delight.
All credit to this simple dish:
May God preserve the British fish.

Poetics

Eschew

I will eschew rhyme.
Rhyme confines, constricts, tidies up.
Experience is not tidy.
Poetry is order – ordering words, images, rhythms.
But where is the order in living?
I will eschew rhyme and neatness and regularity.
I will eschew poetry in order to celebrate disorder.
This is my manifesto. Is it a poem?

Boundary

To set a boundary on speculation
You fix on the physical. This light rain. This damp pavement.
That post-office van drawing up at the corner with its
    official redness.
This and that. Concrete observation
Focuses the moment, defines the self.
I am someone watching this light rain, this damp pavement,
    that red van.
Are all my hopes, ambitions, brave intentions
Shrunk to this little measure?
For the moment, yes.

Try Again

I cannot lose the old iambic flow:
The words assemble thus without my care.
Stop it! rhythms of life and thought and feeling
Move in unpredictable patterns.
Let's have irregular clumps. Shift pauses.
Stumble deliberately sometimes, trying for reality.
And name things properly: that empty chair
Looking at me sideways by the desk.
Consider the uppity impertinence of things.
Point! Describe! Show forth! Manifest!
A yellow lampshade by the typewriter table,
In the corner a filing-cabinet, one drawer half open.
It's you I'm talking to,
You newspaper, you bookcase, you globe of the world
    standing on a little table.
Tell me about yourselves.

Much

Inasmuch
As I do not use the word forasmuch,
As much as some of my forebears
And inasmuch
As I wish to clarify my speech of lumpy words,
I wrap you up, inasmuch,
Together with your friend forasmuch,
Tie you together in a neat, neat parcel
And post it to – Where?
Australia? New Zealand? Antarctica?
Much of a muchness.

Perhaps

Perhaps it may seem
That the Imagists were right,
That hard, clear, precise images
Falling like dropped stones on the path of perception
Are best for poetry. Perhaps
Words like perhaps that have no visual impact
Are otiose. Oh, but otiose
Is itself a word of such velvety suggestion
And 'perhaps'
Sums up all our future imperfects
With such grammatical niceness.
Remember how Virgil used 'forsan'?
Perhaps you had a classical education
Or perhaps you have an antique English cast of mind
And prefer 'mayhap'.
Are you with me?
Perhaps!

Notes for a History of Poetry

When Memory's Fabled Daughter
Descended to the Word,
The lapping sound of water
Was profitably heard.
Through language set in motion
By river, stream, or ocean
Men acted their devotion,
Both tragic and absurd.

Absurdity was troubling:
See now the poet's task:
Leave histrionic doubling
To don a simpler mask.
Winds of the world were nipping:
The bardic robe was slipping:
The poet wanders, sipping
The sad, hypnotic flask.

Now tipsy with suggestion
He staggers on alone,
Resolving every question
To solipsistic moan.
The voice was human, therefore
We credited its flaws:
Now it's the blanks we care for
And listen for the pause.

Then crossed with this deflation
Came ironies of style,
The tone of conversation,
The squint sardonic smile.
Then 'Sir' declines to 'Mister',
And 'Mister' falls to 'Bud';
The hail becomes a whisper,
The rocks dissolve to mud,
Which purifies to water
In critical amend,
And memory's fabled daughter
Is Silence in the end.

Rhymes

If ever you see an eager beaver
Working away in furious fever
Or if you see a Border Reiver
(Old-fashioned kind of high achiever)
Or if you hear a true believer
Warning of Satan, old deceiver,
Or think of Kipling's *Danny Deever*
Or Lizzie Borden with her cleaver
Or if you see a black retriever
Nipping the legs of a coal heaver
Or the official Court Receiver
Sealing the fate of a bankrupt weaver –
Those, I should think, would be the times
When life resolved itself in rhymes.

Word Process

The action of a body of persons
Going or marching along
In orderly succession.
So the dictionary defines 'procession'.
A body of words
Going or marching along
In orderly succession
Might be the definition of a poem.
Is the poet then
A word processor
And is the ubiquitous electronic device
Now used by so many writers
A guaranteed creator
Of word processions,
Of poems?
But when the poet proceeds to write a poem
The process is quite unpredictable,
Nor does he know just what he wants to do.
A procession knows where it is going,
A word processor obeys preceding orders,
The poet creates a world
He had not dreamt of till he found it there,
His own surprised creation.

Words, Words, Words

He talked of language, using words
To describe words. Prospero taught speech to Caliban
Who learned to curse, knowing nothing
Of deep structures or transformational grammar.
About it and about we go, talking
About talking. Let me introduce
Our speaker. Ladies and Gentlemen!
There now, I have defined you, using the vocative.
Friends, Romans, countrymen,
My fellow Americans.
Comrades.
Brethren.
Let me introduce the speaker,
Homo sapiens, uttering utterances.
How these mouthings define us:
Definitely!

Ambition

If I should dedicate my pen
To Daniel in the lions' den
Or if I should re-tell the tale
Of Prophet Jonah and the Whale,
Or once again narrate the story
Of Solomon in all his glory
Or show how skilful modern prose is
Able to tell the tale of Moses:
If I could write a modern fable
Of Adam and Eve, of Cain and Abel,
Or if I could perhaps aspire
To the rapt poetry of Isaiah,
I would presumably be fit
To write a sort of Holy Writ
And would – what fortune could be brighter? –
Become a sort of Holy Writer.

Against Rhyme

I think that if I had the time
I'd write a poem lacking rhyme,
For to a conscientious bard
Verse without rhyme is really hard.
Rhyme neatly tidies up the space
And runs you at a spanking pace,
It feeds you notions one by one
And keeps your fancy running on.
But lacking rhyme you have to find
Deep patterns far within your mind
And weave them into subtle forms
Transcending all established norms
With dialectics of a kind
That rhymesters rarely have in mind.
Rhyming requires no special fitness
As these galumphing lines can witness.
Discerning readers will feel sure a
Case is here of *sprezzatura*,
An old Italian term to style
Self-deprecation done with guile.

Observations

Conductors

Tram conductors used to have machines
Strapped to their chests and issued tickets
With a musical 'ping', a penny one,
A tuppenny or even a threepenny.
Progress has ended that.
On buses I see no conductors,
Give exact fare to the driver,
Who presses buttons, pushes levers,
And then re-starts the bus.
The old conductors fumbled for change
In leather bags worn over the shoulder
And counted out the coins into your palm,
Balancing like seamen as the tram lurched on.
Driving a tram was easy,
The rails carrying you where they led,
But the conductor,
Weighted and freighted with contraptions,
Choosing a ticket – each with its separate colour –
Fitting the proper space to his machine,
Punching the hole exactly,
Climbing upstairs and downstairs on the swaying tram,
Had a harder time.
Children went anywhere for a penny,
A yellow ticket. Red for a tuppenny,
Blue for a threepenny.
Those chromatic journeys
Live in my memory like true adventures,
True adventure stories,
The conductor always the hero.

Roads

Long ago
There was a lane led past a paper-mill:
The smell was quite precise.
Beyond, the beach and freedom.
Afterwards,
Lovers' Lane loitered towards Blackford Hill,
Walked through with picnic sandwiches and lemonade
Consumed by whin bushes.
The hush of those arrested summer streets,
Lilac, laburnum, espaliered apple trees
On the walled gardens.
The coal-carts lumbered into Melville Terrace
From Marchmont Road.
Lothian Road, with Herbert Wiseman's children's concerts
In Usher Hall. There were roads
That led to places; came from places, or were simply there.
There was the Radical Road round Arthur's Seat.

In streets you emphasised the name,
GEORGE Street, QUEEN Street, PRINCES Street,
In roads, the name unstressed, the fact of road gets emphasis,
Newington ROAD, Morningside ROAD, Forrest ROAD,
And so with lane and row and crescent
(Heriot ROW but DARNAWAY Street).
I have no memories that account for this.
It must go back to Roman times, to Roman *strata*,
As in Watling Street.
Let it be figured out by some Roads Scholar.

Yet roads are longer, linking town to town,
Streets are within the town, with grocery shops,
Stationers, drysalters, greengrocers,
And of course houses, houses, windows and front doors,
Curtains, privacies, gentilities.

What we have done to get from place to place!
General Wade built Scottish roads for soldiers,
John Loudon McAdam made with stones and tar,
Ways to and from, along and through,
All paved with good intentions,
Till the last word in means of moving,
Replacing devious routes, unwinding motorways.
We are told in Genesis
That fallen man was cursed with need to work:
That primal curse
ROAD WORKS.

Walls

Stone in the north, bricks in the softer south.
The dry-stane dyke, first sign of northern marches,
And then so many walls with massive stone,
Some circling miles round privileged estates,
Apple trees leaning over walls, suggesting privacy
Behind. Some walls with broken glass on top
Rebuffing keelie children, showing that walls enclose
And don't invite. Yet walls can be inviting,
Even stone walls, as you explore looking for entry gate,
With flowers on show and teas, walls protecting
Shared social demonstrations. Thanks, courteous wall.

Brick walls suggest English suburban gardens,
Neat, self-contained and private. Or the English
    country-house
With high brick walls enclosing generations
Of garden planning, and a well designed
Perspective, a lake, perhaps, a ha-ha even,
Brown showing his Capability.

Perimeter walls, unfriendly modern invasions
Round prisons or military sites, with spikes, barbed wire,
More terrible than the broken bottle glass
Preventing climbers.

Mellow brick walls have charm and history,
But the stone wall – stones dressed or undressed,
    proper or en déshabille,
Is the true wall for me.
Stone walls do not a prison make; they make,
Eloquent and visible, a recall
Of human habitation and design,
Of rolling years, of you and me
And all our varied and perplexing pasts.

Bridges

A stone arch is the simplest
Crossing a Highland burn or straddling a country road
    in Fife.
The great geometrical Forth Bridge with its familiar
    triangles
Flanked by the flowing road-bridge with ribbons
    of traffic,
Little wooden bridges across trickles of water,
Repeating arches of viaducts bracketing distant banks,
Simple trotting of the long bridge over the Tay
Beside the ghost of the great disaster.
The high suspension bridge at Clifton,
Westminster Bridge where Wordsworth wrote his sonnet,
Le pont d'Avignon where they danced.
The sad tourists' bridge at Venice:
Let's try this one for Sighs.

A pier, said Stephen, is a disappointed bridge,
A failure to communicate,
A statement made with none to receive.
Bridges of language, flung across fathomless gaps,
Person to person, most difficult bridge of all,
Like tossing a rope from ship to shore:
Have you caught it? Is it made fast?
Do I reach you? Do you follow me?
Or shall we meet at the middle coming from
    different directions?
Arches of words may simply stand
As ornaments, not joiners.
We can play games with building stones,
But the old message haunts us:
Only connect.

Water

Life comes from water, and a little
In a single malt whisky releases the natural oils.
Peat-coloured burn water descends the Highland brae,
Lucent lake water laps,
The endless ocean rolls – rolls on, as Byron told it to.
Acqua minerale graces Italian tables.
Salt water covers most of the planet earth.

A glass of water held in the hand:
A pill plops in.
For this relief much thanks.
The watering can sprays patterns on the flower bed.
The indiscriminate garden hose ejects its rising flow.

A child in the bath
Plashes and plays, with bobbing plastic duck.
Loofahs bring water roughly to the skin.
Rain falls, not mainly on the plains:
Gosh, I got *drenched*.
Water gurgles down gutters after storm.

What is this curse, this blessing,
That plays its terrible games? We pray for it
And pray for it to cease.
We perish equally in drought and flood.

I don't care, said Noah,
If I never see water again.
And he made wine from grapes, got drunk,
Disgraced himself.
But left a lovely legacy.

Squares

How right the angles, how neat and boxed the shape!
No nonsense about these corners, foursquare they are.
You don't see them on trees or flowers
But in the chessboard patterns made by men
In hedgerowed fields. Streets too can be squared
With gardens in the middle. Noughts and crosses
Go in squares.
And those cross words that addicts puzzle out.
Square brackets, now, that tidy words away
Discreetly in parenthesis
Suggest a mind unsquare, not neatly patterned,
Full of left-overs; not left over, though,
From a square meal, downed with brisk appetite
By hungry sailors on a square-rigged ship.
Not much imagination lies in square,
Mindless square-bashing, or going bemused
Back to square one.
Try to fit a square peg in a round hole, though,
And you'll need care and cunning,
Misfits provoking second thoughts
That threaten neatness.
I think of truffle hounds truffling and snuffling
As though digging for square roots.

Circles

Each point is equidistant from the centre.
If you move forward on it you return
To where you started. What a perfect
Symbol of vanity. No thought of that
When holding childish hands in ring-a-roses
We circled, sang and dropped. Or circled round
A centre child,
Here's a poor widow she's left alone,
Or later, in the eightsome reel
Facing your bounding partner.
Hoops, crowns, rings, the equator itself,
Toys, symbols, signs, devices,
Roundness is all.
O the exclamatory circle! O, O!
Performed with rounded lips. Performed
In Shakespeare's wooden O, encircled actors
Busy exclaiming to a circle audience.
I see the sewing circle sitting round,
Domestic, tame. No vicious circle this
Like that where Roman emperors
Threw Christians to the lions.
Here we go round the mulberry bush,
The circuit judge,
The milkman on his rounds,
The millwheel turned by water,
The circulation of the blood, Harvey's discovery,
The circulation war of newspapers.
'Tis love that makes the world go round,
With this ring I thee and thou,
With this ring,
With this circle . . .

Shall I leave it on, sir? Yes, let it stay
Hugging the finger as the flesh decays,
Rolled round in earth's diurnal course –
Not the eternity we thought of once.

Lines

Consider it along these lines.
Lines of communication, like railways, telephone wires,
Or those military ones you must secure before you
    advance further,
Or lines an actor must remember not to forget,
Or the hundred lines required of the errant schoolboy,
Or the marriage lines that make an honest woman,
Or the bottom line where everything stops like
    the buck at the White House,
Or the dotted line where you sign and commit yourself,
Or the line you toe, afraid to go off limits.
Mostly however lines are joiners
Stretching from here to there
And if they are parallel
Never meeting
However far they are produced in either direction.
Strange that lines are joiners but parallel lines
    never meet,
Always side by side though,
Running along singing a song side by side.
Wishing I had a nice line in wit
I write these few lines
About lines.

Things

So many. Objects clutter the world,
Creations of *homo faber*. Left to itself
What would the world have? Let me see,
Trees of course, flowers, grass, rocks, sand.
Beavers build dams, bower-birds build their bowers,
And other creatures make their special dwellings.
But *homo faber* goes in for things, fabricated objects.
Cans, condoms, bottles, bags, to mention only some
That litter our parks and beaches.
Indoors there are corkscrews, cutlery, cups and saucers,
Shoes, shaving-cream,
Pepper-pots, candle-snuffers, pencils, soap, tea-towels,
Variety to boggle the mind. Think of them
Occupying spaces, standing, lying, falling, being handled,
Used, abused, bought, sold, discarded,
Given as presents, fought over,
Left in legacies, or simply left.
Think of the factories producing things
(It's an awfully ticklish job, said Gracie,
Making a thing for a thingummy-bob).
A retired seaman assembles a ship in a bottle,
Someone builds the Taj Mahal out of matches,
Ingenious devices are invented
To help us do things we do not need to do.
Think of shop windows and the cabinets
Of connoisseurs, Victorian chamber pots in antique dealers.
What hath man wrought?
The world is so full of a number of things, said RLS,
I'm sure we should all be as happy as kings.
But who said kings were happy?

Sky

Is God up there with all his heavenly host?
Freckled or plain, azure or white or dark,
Overhead scenery shifting. What is the play?
Who wrote it? Has it a happy ending?
Jacob dreamt of a ladder ascending there,
With angels moving up and down
Like workmen with pails, going about their business.
Astronauts have seen no ladder, no, nor heavenly throne,
But they were trained for other observations.
What can we see? What do we want to see?
Pie in the sky? Stars telling our fortunes?
Father Wishart in Heaven?
Rolled with our little planet
We see sun rise, sun set, moon in its phases,
Patterns of heavenly hosts.
Lie on your back in the grass and watch
Clouds passing and changing shape.
Worlds of imagination flow from sky to brain.
Messages? Aerograms?
Perhaps. For sky is not mere space,
Not just a context for astronomers,
But our umbrella, inevitable,
Our roof, definer of our upward observation
In daily and nightly goings and comings.
Our scripture, too, where we read mysteries,
Our threat, our comforter.
Are all these messages just jokes,
Sky larks invented by an unknown jester
To make us laugh or cry?
I speculate no further:
The sky's the limit.

Earth

Plunge your fingers in it on a warm spring day,
You feel the nurture, the stir of mothering.
See what emerges! Snowdrops, crocuses, daffodils,
Precursors of hosts, multicoloured, multiform.
We engage with earth, plant in it, plough it,
Coax it, bully it, and in the end
Consign ourselves to it.
Adam means earth, red earth,
His punishment to till it, master it.
But no, we cannot master it,
It sulks or broods or yields
Or left alone splairges into such wildness
We stand in awe.
Walk on it barefoot, feel the naked sole
Treading on Mother Earth. Antaeus
To keep his strength had to touch down on Earth.
O we may build on it
Cover it with structures housing our desires,
Smother with paving all its crumbly warmth;
But see – suburban gardens behind ribbon dwellings,
Earth preserved, redeemed, venerated.
Look from the aircraft, endless patterns of fields
Mock our new artefacts.
It is there, earth, the worms remake it,
It keeps its primal smell.
We are all earthlings. Earth is our heritage.
Heaven we imagine but we stand on earth,
The primal substance, trying to answer
The primal question:
What on earth are we doing here?

Sea-Changes

Bays, estuaries, beaches, rocks.
All round the coast
The varied ocean heaves and laps.
We are an island
Oppressed (redeemed?) by water
Circumjacent,
Ringed round by wrecks invisible,
Fishing boats, trading vessels, transports.
Julius Caesar, William the Conqueror,
Walter Scott sailing from Leith to Edinburgh
Or on his 1814 lighthouse trip,
Small lobster craft from Pittenweem,
Drifters from Ullapool or Peterhead,
Thames barges, tea clippers,
The great Armada swept to the north by storms,
Wives and children maist despairing
Watching doomed rock-bound boats
Without Grace Darling. Sea-girt
This island. In the night
Waves breaking on the shore awake no sleeper,
Rhythm of their restless movement
By habitude half-heard, unheeded.
And then
Seaside resorts, bathing machines once,
Sea-side landlady and martello tower,
Joke juxtaposition, yet how strange,
How strange the coastal prospect,
The sea-history,
How sad the break-break-break
On the cold grey stones,
And for Keats's pure ablution
Round these human shores
Pollution.

Reflections

Orpheus and Eurydice

I wonder now,
If Orpheus hadn't looked back, but just kept chatting,
Eyes front, but talking backwards,
He could perhaps have kept the bond unbroken
Until they reached sunlight.
What was it like down there? Have you read
Any good books lately? What shall we do
Tomorrow? I know a nice place
For lunch. Knowing she was listening
He would have kept her real, kept them both real,
Rebuilding little intimacies.
Love is like that.

Demand and Supply

The white page.
No, not satin-clad small boy attendant at wedding,
Though he indeed is a subject for musing,
But this white page on which I write
Producing black hieroglyphics that march to the margin.
The white page pleads, exhorts, demands,
Do something to redeem my blankness.
So, white page, I make you maculate
With this small song that climbed into my head
The other morning as I lay in bed.
   O do not curse
   The universe
   In prose or verse
   However terse.
   It might be better,
   But it could be worse.
Are you happier now?

Fromaging

Fromaging, we used to say when we were young,
Is to forage for cheese and other snacky lunchy things,
Opening cupboard doors in kitchens, seek and ye shall find.
O young fromageurs, privileged fridge-peekers,
What sudden sardines surprise you,
What portions of pâté,
What relishy remnants
Reveal themselves to your canny questing?
Hunters and gatherers, we are told,
Were our ancestors once. And now,
Safely searching in heated houses,
Cruising in comfort through cast-off cuisine,
We collect comestibles.
Thoroughly civilised we are, thoroughly civilised.

Cherub

'The cherub,' the old lady said
Of the male infant sleeping in his pram
Outside the post-office.
She thought of little chubby cupids
With tiny wings – not what King David meant
When he saw the Lord rise upon a cherub
And fly upon the wings of the wind,
Nor what Ezekiel visioned,
When the stone like sapphire and the cloud and the fire
Spoke of God's glory while four-faced cherubim
Stretched their enormous wings and turned to wheels,
Great angelic figures, heralds and outriders
Of God himself, symbols of power and holiness
And mystery, perhaps of terror. And they stood
At the door of the east gate of the Lord's house
With divine glory shed over them.
How are the mighty fallen?
But Wordsworth saw the infant
Trailing clouds of glory
And so uniting
Muling and pewking with Ezekiel's vision.
It takes a poet, I suppose,
To see the lady's cherub in the prophet's.

Principles

Some people stand on them. Some people lack them.
(One should object to that in principle.)
In differing inventions
The principle may remain the same.
A man of principle is principled.
The principles of morals, now, are something
Philosophers have long debated. Freud
Ventured beyond the pleasure principle
And told us what he found.
We should return perhaps
To first principles.
But what were those?

Pigs

'And pigs perform in perpetuity.'
These were the words that came into my head
As I lay dozing. These were the words,
The Holy Book begins, spoken by Moses
To all Israel. Deuteronomy one.
But my piggish words
Positing everlasting acts by unclean creatures?
Whence and wherefore? Who was pronouncing?
Flotsam and jetsam of our vast subconscious
Emerge mysteriously, I know.
But pigs perform in perpetuity?
Then I remembered
I had been reading
About the eighteenth-century learned pigs
Taught to do tricks by showmen.
Learned pigs, they were called.
Well
I thought of certain members of the Bar,
My learned friend, hired by a miscreant
To save his bacon.

Elemental

A little water releases the natural oils,
So into the *uisge beatha*, water of life,
Goes aqua pura but just a modicum
And we sit with glass in hand by the fire.
Fire and water, primal elements
In the old theory, with earth and air the others.
Air we breathe, earth we observe when walking in the
    country,
But here with fire and water, in my own element as it
    were,
We shed the burden of time.
Domestic, protected, anticipating,
Crowning the day.
Straw-coloured, still, reflective,
The liquid beckons from our glasses,
I nose, I taste, I swallow.
Outside the earth revolves, the sun drops slowly,
But here the still centre holds us
Elemental with fire and water.

Weirdo

The man was a weirdo
If ever there was one.
A particoloured scarf wound round his neck,
    a squashed bonnet on his head
And a patter of incomprehensible words
    addressed to passers by.
A weirdo,
A daftie.
We mean of course that we don't understand
    what he's up to
And that frightens us rather.

Inst., Ult. and Prox.

Inst. and ult. are now in desuetude.
Answering yours of the 14th ult.
Referring to a meeting of the 20th inst.
I see a legal gent, wing-collared,
In a brown Victorian office, whiskered perhaps,
Insting and ulting and proxing, playing with dates.
All gone, all the arrangements
Long deranged by time.
Consider wills now, testaments,
Willed benefactions of an earlier age,
Old testaments framed by long dead testators.
Shakespeare bequeathed to his wife his second-best bed.
Will Shakespeare they called him, appropriately.
There's something very ult about a will,
Ultimate statement. That last second-best bed,
Proxime accessit.

Food of Love?

He flicked a switch. Out popped a voice,
Vox pop. His poppa's voice? His Master's voice?
A pop group? Anyway, a sound investment.
Be not afraid, the isle is full of noises.
But there's the rub: too full, too full of noises,
Accessible by switching. Yet have I silence left,
The poet said, the croon of a'.
If musak be the food of love, play on.
It isn't. Switch off.

Oxtail Soup

The tail was on a living creature once,
Twirling and swishing. Or think of chicken soup
Or the humble sausage. Boiling or frying we transmogrify
Our fellow creatures. What a way to live!
Well, nature is red in tooth and claw,
All life is medium rare, and who can say
When all the recipes are acted out,
'Well done, thou good and faithful servant'?
Dishonest clerks may sometimes cook the books:
Where are the diet police to book the cooks?

Banana

That proverbial banana skin.
Have you actually seen someone slip on one?
Would you laugh?
Ha ha, he has slipped on the proverbial banana skin,
Ho ho, he has proved the truth of the proverb.
Are bananas really so treacherous?
Couldn't you slip just as easily on something else?
Slicing a banana into fruit salad
I pose such questions.
Do you shoot yourself in the foot?
Do you kick your own goal?
Are you perhaps your own worst enemy?
Are you maybe too clever for your own good?
Eat your banana, my friend, and put the skin
In the dustbin.

Fog

Fog will return tonight, he said,
Busy with the map on the screen,
He knows.
I listen to the mouthings of politicians,
Their wind will not disperse the fog.
I look at the globe on my desk:
There is Russia. There is China. Huge, huge. Turn it
   round
And there is America. Wasps and Latins,
Hewers of wood in the Amazon forest,
Residual Indians,
Miners, majors, money-makers,
Street children, chickens running and fried,
Porch gossip in the Midwest. Wiseacres in Washington.
Turn it round again.
Nicotine-stained fingers of writers in Budapest,
A barman polishes glasses in Chelsea,
Huddled talk in the Kremlin.
Yes, fog will return tonight
And stay tomorrow. In this thickness
(As Theseus once remarked)
How easy is a Bush supposed a Bear.

Afterthoughts

Streaks

Observation with extensive view
Said Dr Johnson, not numbering the streaks of the tulip.
Streaks of the tulip! What did he see
In his mind's eye when he used that phrase?
A tulip, streaked, stands sharply out
While all mankind from China to Peru
Blur in a chain or do a strip-the-willow
Or lose themselves in anthropology.
Short-sighted he was, streaked tulips
Were too difficult. Mankind's the thing:
The mind copes, not the eye. Just representation
Of general nature, he said.
Like
Parallel straight lines
Are straight lines
On the same plane
That never meet
However far
They are produced
In either direction.
But parallel lines do meet in the end
Our universe being what we now know it is,
And just representation
Is unjust
And mankind
Is man-unkind.
And Dr Johnson
Wise, humane, sensible Dr Johnson
Was really, as Boswell showed, unique.
Observation with intensive view
Showed all his streaks.
It is the streakiness that we remember.

Artificial

Jubilant in corner
The multicoloured flowers rise from the vase.
Don't water them, she said, they're artificial.
Who would have thought it? Cunningly formed they are,
Deceiving the eye that knows these colours,
These shapes, these rising stems,
This eloquent chromatic balancing,
As Nature's burgeoning. But no,
They're made of silk.
I saw three lunch-time yuppies in a pub,
Suitably suited, balanced on their stools,
Ascending towards their glasses.
Don't water them, I almost told the barmaid,
They're artificial. Not of silk, perhaps,
But something smooth and plausible.
Don't misunderstand me: flowers of silk
I find attractive. Artificial men
Perhaps less so, but still
Giving a certain pleasure to observers.
On the whole, though, I prefer the flowers.

Funny

Misdemeanours of politicians, anguish of nations,
Scandals, cruelties, confusions,
Stuff of crafted headlines.
As long as you keep your sense of humour,
The hostess smiled at the dinner guests.
Chomp chomp, slurp slurp, they were sensing humorously
Mudlands of politics, miseries of foreigners,
Distant dooms.
A funny thing happened to me the other day
Going down the garden path:
The laughing flowers nodded in the wind
Exhaling scents of humour.

Time

There were olden times. Story-books showed knights
In armour. There were Pharaohs, Emperors, Kings,
And Peasants of course, who tilled the soil
And sometimes revolted.
Times changed. Slowly in childhood, waiting
For the end of school, the summer holidays,
Or only Friday, heralding the week-end.
In time, one felt time moving faster,
Years ebbing away so fast, another date,
A later number.
You prepositioned time: in time, on time,
    not before time, once upon a time,
You could save time, do time, spare time,
    beat time, kill time even,
There were part time and full time and overtime.
And all the time it moves.
Pondering over time – a way of wasting time, perhaps –
You end ahead of where you started,
For the ticking kept on, keeps on,
'Not yet' becomes 'already',
You are trapped in the flow, released
Some time, some future point
Which waits, waits, waits,
Already there but not arrived,
Some future point when time will stop for you
And all the moving pictures of your life
Stand still at last, frozen in one cartoon.

You will not read it. But I write this now
To say I know it will be there,
Rather it will have been there,
Some future perfect waits,
However imperfect the present, some day it *will have been*,
Lying in ordered sequence.
In God's mind? In circumambient air?
And what of me?
I shall know in time, perhaps,
Time out of mind, mind out of time.
Time: mind how you go.

Not Gray's Elegy

After street riots comes the curfew.
Stay inside. Lock your doors. Terror stalks outside.
Far from the rural scene of Thomas Gray
Whose curfew tolled the knell of parting day
The curfew tolls the knell of people shot
In streets and pubs and shops
Because, like Mount Everest, they were there.
The gunman homeward sneaks his cunning way
And leaves the world to darkness.

Balconies

A balcony is the best suspension.
High above pavement we command the scene:
Secure, serene, on our wrought-iron stand
We raise our glasses. Summer evening drinks
Are best on balconies. But there are other uses,
Other pleasures, other dangers.
Juliet had her balcony and many a lover
Has climbed to one or scrambled down from one,
And many a lonely scholar
Has leant on balcony rail, sadly observing.
I have seen balconies
In Edinburgh's New Town,
Douce, quietly respectable, no mad escapes
From there or lovers' leaps. Mediterranean balconies
In courtyards, or outside bedroom windows towards the sea.
How many scenes in film or theatre
Have linked the balcony to deeds of passion,
Actions of high romance.

But I remember
Sipping an evening grappa on a balcony
In Genoa with you while the storm raged
And lightning lit the sky.
I see it now a symbol of our life
Together, suspended in mutual love,
Facing a raging world.
Now you are gone I look for balconies,
Symbols of lost content.

Seasons

Write about the seasons, she said.
Well, you can't beat Keats for Autumn.
And what about Spring time, the only pretty ring time,
And Summer is icumen in?
But I could start with Genesis 8:22,
'While the earth remaineth
Seedtime and harvest and cold and heat
And summer and winter
And day and night
Shall not cease.'
A threat or a promise?
A promise surely: not for me
Adam's seasonless paradise,
The languorous pleasures of a prelapsarian garden,
Blossom and fruit together on the tree,
Never a worm in the always full-blown rose.
Ah the changes, the changes!
Chill rain slants down on bent pedestrian heads,
Umbrellas take to the air,
Scraping of feet on doorstep mat
Returning to a warm and walled protection,
Food, books, talk, a large malt whisky.

Roll round to sleepy sunning on the beach
With little curling waves plashing
As the calm tide nudges in,
And sand in sandwiches.
Only weeks later from the harbour wall
I watch the frenzied breakers pound the rocks
As golden autumn turns to beckon winter
With equinoctial gales.
Welcome, gales and tempests,
Rousing glories of climate, whistling sharp and clean.
Roll round to daffodils that come before the swallow dares
To early green on trees
Not yet encumbered with the summer's dust.
Memory, hope, desire, regret,
Look back, look forward,
All that mixed texture of the searching mind
That keeps us human. Backward through flipping seasons
To ante-natal blank: forward with young desires
The best is yet to be – till, startled,
We look at death.
I cannot think of any better way.

Lightning

Lightning illuminates the landscape
In sudden flashes. A stark tree here
Vividly black; part of a stone wall there
Old and silent.
So I see you suddenly, reading on the couch
Legs curled underneath you, snapshot
Of memory. Behind there is the French window
Leading into the garden. Such lightning pictures,
Fragments of many years, so much being and doing,
Show me how long you have been dead.
Once it was you, there; you could smile
    and say something.
Now I grope for the flashes.
I cannot prolong them, cannot ever
Give them a living movement and a voice.
The stillness I can bear, even the evanescence.
It is the voice I miss.

Descent

The children kept on sledging into the dusk,
Down, down the slope that borders the Bow Butts.
Down, down they went, laughing and shrieking,
The white snow, the black trees, the Bruegel
   landscape.
They had to trudge up, trailing their sledges,
Before the next descent. Descent of children.
   Descent of man.
Thank God for gravity; it sends them down,
Rejoicing in descent. They re-enact the Fall.
Yellow lights on the path above the slope
Illumined their descent as darkness came.
Light. Fall. Darkness. We make it our business
To fall from light to dark. We want it. We love it.
Far off in the Gulf they are preparing for war,
Tanks rehearse in the desert, in sand, not snow,
But here in this Scottish village the children
Descend the snowy slopes with laughter into darkness.

Progress

'Further than that I cannot go.'
These words were in my head as I woke up.
Further than what? Was I announcing
That I had reached my limits?
What limits?
In what direction is my progress blocked?
Was I announcing
Completion of achievement, taking pride
In having gone so far? Was I regretting
Failing powers? Or insurmountable obstacles?
Am I a satisfied power?
No. The truth recedes,
The sceptic in one grows. But scepticism
Is knowledge of the difficulties, no resting place.
Into the wilderness then, though who will send
Manna and quails I do not know, nor whether
There is a Promised Land.
I haven't forty years, though. Perhaps my waking words
Meant I should stop and cultivate a garden
Here where I find myself. A garden in the wilderness
Warding surrounding chaos?
A fine thought for an old man.

The Stopped Clock

I forgot to wind the clock. It stands at four,
Unticking. The time is really after six,
Recorded time, that is – but not on this clock.
It stands there, silent reminder
Of the still point of the turning world.
Can I climb into it
Like Alice through the looking-glass,
Entering that timeless world
To escape from that perpetual merging
Of the already into the not yet?
Can I? Here, now, sitting in my chair, my feet
   on the rug,
My pen in my hand, watching the stopped clock,
I know that question will be answered
Sooner or later, later or sooner,
When this moment, all moments,
Must slip into silence and my counting brain
Will stop. Time will be conquered then, for me at least.

Flowers and Grocers

I took him for a drive in the car
When he was ninety-two, I less than half that.
He marvelled at the daffodils come round again,
And he still here. 'Look,' he said, 'daffodils.'
Is old age comforted by spring's return
Or do we see renewal as for nature
And not for us? He was alive for one more spring
At least. The cruelty of that indifference
Was felt by me and not by him.
I thought instead of how when we are gone
The round of life continues, grass and flowers and people,
Buds appear, grow fat, burst out,
People follow their daily rounds, intent
On their own trivialities. Couples court by the river
As though they were immortal and unique.
He broke into these thoughts with exclamation.
'Look,' he said, reading a village shop-sign slowly,
'J. Thomson, family grocer.'
He smiled, and said again 'J. Thomson
Family grocer. He is a
Family grocer,' he told me,
Earnest and pleased. 'J. Thomson, family grocer.
That's nice,' he added, settling in his seat,
Touched by the ordinariness.
I felt ashamed and moved. Why should this simple sign
Of undistinguished human dailiness
Have touched him so?
Ninety-two he was, not long for this world,
This world of daffodils and family grocers.
Now myself well past the Psalmist's span
Of seventy years I often think of this
And feel, surprisingly, a surge of love
For flowers and grocers everywhere.

Not the Departure Lounge

They've checked your passport, screened you through security,
And here, in the departure lounge, you wait.
No man's land it is, unreachable now
The set familiar world you left behind.
And yet – the plane's delayed? What does that sign say?
How long do we stay here
Betwixt and between?

He said he was in the departure lounge of life,
Past the divide, waiting for his flight.
And I, who am older, cannot accept that.
True, the flight may be called
At any time. But not cut off
From my familiar world, my passport shown, my bag X-rayed.
I come and go at will, my littered desk
Still there, my books on shelves.
The morning post with all its silly clamour
Arrives and claims attention,
A Haydn quartet on the radio,
And you come to the study offering coffee.
No; not a departure lounge.
Though I may go at any time
Right now I am still here,
Part of my always world,
And we can talk, discussing what to eat and drink
Tonight, or laughing
At some daft incident we both recall.
In the midst of life we are in death of course,
But in the midst of life, not the departure lounge,
As this warm scribe my hand affirms.

Finale

Nel mezzo del cammin di nostra vita
He wrote. Half way through life; a youngster.
And I well past three score and ten
Beyond the span for Dante and the Bible
Look back now, having shared
No Hell in Auschwitz, reached no Heaven certainly.
And Purgatory? These three states
Are not my categories. Lucky survivor,
I have come through, incredulous,
Untouched except in thought and sympathy
By all that nightmare.
I have known love and safety
While others went to torture and to death.
And I write poems.
Poetry makes nothing happen, Auden said.
Perhaps. The shapers of our fate,
The loud-mouthed politicians, plotters, planners,
Manipulators, seekers after power,
Are moved by forces I can not compute.
Good fortune left me out of tragedy.
Good fortune? History's outsider,
Sitting reflective in my study
I write poems.
Do I guard
The civilization that they suffered for,
Culture, compassion, wit, amusement?
We are not amused
At jackboot savagery or swastikas.
Are we sitting comfortably?

The poisoned past infects the present still,
And as we sit and talk over our glasses
This autumn evening with the daylight fading,
Lucky survivors, what are we to say
To the dead sufferers?
What are we to tell our grandchildren?
Hope, I suppose, is what sustains us,
Against the odds, but hope,
But hope, but hope.
Otherwise just the dark.